BUFFALO GALS

BUFFALO GALS
WOMEN of the OLD WEST

BRANDON MARIE MILLER

Lerner Publications Company • Minneapolis

With love to Paul, Jolene,
and Justin

Page 2: Colorado zoologist Martha Maxwell

Library of Congress Cataloging-in-Publication Data

Miller, Brandon Marie.
    Buffalo gals : women of the old West / by Brandon Marie Miller.
       p. cm.
    Includes bibliographical references and index.
    ISBN 0-8225-1730-2
    1. Women pioneers–West (U.S.)–History–Juvenile literature.
2. West (U.S.)–History–Juvenile literature. [1. Pioneers. 2. Women–
Biography. 3. Frontier and pioneer life. 4. West (U.S.)–History.]
I. Title.
F596.M537 1994
978'.02–dc20
                                        94-5063
                                         CIP
                                         AC

Manufactured in the United States of America
1 2 3 4 5 6 – I/JR – 00 99 98 97 96 95

Contents

MANY A WEARY MILE

I have not told you half we suffered. I am not adequate to the task.

–Elizabeth Smith Geer,
the trail's end, 1847

Not long after sunrise on a May day in 1841, a dozen jam-packed covered wagons rumbled out of a small town along the Missouri River. Ox teams pulled the wagons steadily westward toward the Pacific Coast. Most of the 69 men, women, and children in the party walked alongside the wagons. Dawn rose behind their backs, but tonight the sun would set ahead of them, a sign of hope just over the horizon. They were the first trickle in a flood of pioneers, lured by the promise of a better life in the American West.

An advertisement for California Territory promises: "Land for a Million Farmers."

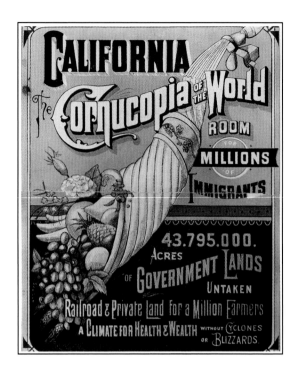

Difficult times pushed many American families to consider moving west. In 1837 the United States slid into an economic depression. Banks closed their doors; thousands of unemployed workers crowded eastern cities. Farm prices plummeted, and many people lost their land. To make matters worse, diseases like yellow fever, typhoid, and tuberculosis ravaged the country year after year.

For people hit squarely by bad times, the West became a symbol of health, wealth, and freedom. "We had nothing to lose," one woman wrote, "and we might gain a fortune." The journals of fur trappers and explorers, reprinted on the East Coast, told of western adventures. Letters from Oregon missionaries also excited trouble-weary Americans. To many readers, the missionaries' tales of religious zeal paled next to their descriptions of rich farmland, timber, fishing, and furs. Societies sprang up encouraging settlement of Oregon Country. California, too, received good reviews, painted as an earthly paradise of sunshine and lush fruit.

The temptation of cheap land in paradise was hard to resist. During the spring of 1842, another 200 people traveled west. A year later, 1,000 optimistic settlers braved the journey. After the 1848 discovery of gold in California, the numbers exploded to 30,000 in 1849 and 55,000 in 1850. Thousands of European immigrants, mainly from Germany, the British Isles, and Scandinavia, joined the hopefuls heading west.

Most pioneers, especially those heading to the goldfields of California, were single men. But families and some single women undertook the western journey, too. Of the 50,000 people heading west in 1852, about 7,000 were women.

Publishers rushed to print manuals like *The National Wagon Road Guide* and *The Emigrants Guide to Oregon and California*. Unfortunately, too many guidebooks proved dangerously unreliable. One manual went so far as to assure readers that any notions of toil, hardship, and danger on the trail were products of their "own fruitful imagination." Although women studied the manuals, the books hardly offered a word of advice for female pioneers. How to cook, clean, dress, camp, and care for children on the long adventure was left for women to discover.

Usually, the man of the household was the one who made the decision to pull up stakes and move the family west. While women shared the hope for a better life, many found it painful to sell their homes and sever ties with friends, community, and relatives. Pushing beyond the established boundaries of the United States, early pioneers were emigrants to a foreign, mostly uncharted land. California and the Southwest belonged to Mexico. The United States and Great Britain both claimed Oregon Country, an area so large it included parts of six future states. But few white people lived there. All the western lands were home to Native American families.

A woman's journey west carried an added burden, coming at a time of life when she might be pregnant or caring for young children. The prospect of abandoning society to face months of heat, dust, storms, and "savage" Indians left many women with misgivings. "I have been reading the various guides of the route to California," wrote Losida Frizzell. "They have not improved my ideas of the pleasure of the trip."

Another woman sang a hymn at her wedding only days before leaving for a "jumping off" spot in Missouri. The lyrics asked:

> Can I bid you farewell?
> Can I leave you,
> Far in heathen lands to dwell?

Not all women looked west reluctantly. One new bride, full of youth and enthusiasm, viewed the trip as an adventure with "castles of shining gold" waiting at the end. And Helen Carpenter, a bride of four months, recorded, "Ho—for California—at last we are on the way and with good luck may some day reach the 'promised land.'" Still other women probably shared Luzena Wilson's bittersweet feelings:

> My husband grew enthusiastic and wanted to start immediately, but I would not be left behind. I thought where he could go I could, and where I went I could take my two little toddling babies. I little realized then the task I had undertaken.

Western emigrants included women and young children.

Once the decision was made, the journey west could be tackled in several ways. Some people booked passage on a ship and sailed around South America to California. Others traveled to Panama, cut across the isthmus, then sailed up the Pacific coast. By the late 1860s, railroads spanned the continent and provided the quickest, if most expensive, way to travel. Without much baggage but themselves, many single women traveling west chose dusty, bumpy stagecoaches. Stage stops along the route offered crowded rooms and meals of questionable quality. Nearly 3,000 Mormon emigrants embarked upon perhaps the most brutal western journey. Between 1856 and 1860, they walked westward, pulling handcarts all the way from Iowa to Utah.

By far the most popular means of family transportation was the oxen-drawn covered wagon. The typical wagon was built of seasoned hardwood, waterproofed with caulk and tar. Finished, it measured about

A wagon train winds west along the Santa Fe Trail.

4 feet wide and 10 to 12 feet long. The wagon had to be large enough to haul roughly 2,500 pounds of supplies, but not too heavy for eight to twelve oxen to pull. A thick canvas covering was rainproofed with oil. Spare parts—axles, wheels, spokes, and wagon tongues—hung beneath the wagon bed. Other necessities lashed to the wagon sides included water barrels, grease buckets, and heavy rope.

After months of preparation, the wagon sat stuffed with tools, cooking ware, clothes, bedding, sewing supplies, guns and ammunition, a few luxuries, and food. Guidebooks recommended each emigrant carry 200 pounds of flour, 150 pounds of bacon, 10 pounds of coffee, 20 pounds of sugar, and 10 pounds of salt. Added to this were staples of dried beans and fruit, rice, tea, pickles, baking soda, cornmeal, and vinegar.

Buying a wagon and oxen and outfitting the whole project cost between $600 and $1,000. Travelers also needed ready cash to buy supplies along the way, pay ferry costs across rivers, and help set up a new home. Seeking the promised lands of the West was not for the very poor.

ACROSS THE WIDE MISSOURI

Travelers, usually in covered wagons, left their homes in eastern states and perched on the edge of white civilization in Missouri River towns, near the head of the Oregon Trail. More than 350,000 pioneers eventually took this main trail west between 1843 and the late 1860s. At places like Independence and Saint Joseph, Missouri, and Council Bluffs, Iowa, emigrants purchased last-minute supplies, made wagon repairs, and sought advice. Families and solo travelers then joined together in large groups for protection on the trail.

The first leg of the Oregon Trail followed the Platte River toward the Rocky Mountains. Oxen plodded over the plains, slowly climbing to South Pass in Wyoming Territory and the Continental Divide—the boundary between eastward and westward flowing waters. Beyond the Rockies, the trail forked into two routes, one continuing northward along the Snake River in Oregon Country (Idaho, today); the offshoot following the Humboldt River heading toward California.

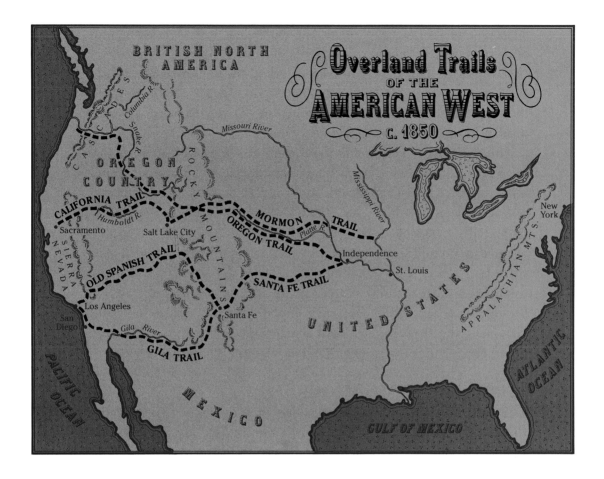

Emigrants to southern California followed the Santa Fe Trail from Missouri to a split near Santa Fe in New Mexico Territory. The Old Spanish Trail carried on to Los Angeles; the Gila River Trail to San Diego. On any route, travel was slow and often boring, with wagon trains covering only 10 to 20 miles each day. One woman reported that most people in her party had lost track of the day of the week. "Still pressing onward," she wrote. "It is a long and tedious journey."

All along the Oregon Trail, emigrants eagerly kept a lookout for landmarks announcing their progress. In Nebraska, diaries noted sightings of Chimney Rock, towering 500 feet overhead, and Scotts Bluff. Just into Wyoming lay Fort Laramie, followed by Independence Rock,

where many pioneers carved their names, and Devil's Gate. Emigrants described antelope and prairie dogs and the excitement of spotting their first herd of buffalo. Most white people had never seen anything like the Great Plains: oceans of tough grass as far as you could see, a huge bowl of sky overhead, and, often, not a tree in sight. Hardly a paradise, the land seemed a fit home only for Indians, the early emigrants thought. Later pioneers, hungry for free land, willingly settled the arid plains stretching from North Dakota down to Texas, and west to parts of Wyoming, Colorado, and Montana.

Guidebooks warned travelers that the journey was "one in which time is every thing." Leaving in spring, when there was grass enough to feed the livestock, settlers raced against the onset of winter more than 2,000 miles to the Pacific Coast. If they delayed for too long, deadly snows might trap them in the mountains that stretched like a wall before Oregon and California.

While the guidebooks reported that the trip would take three or four months, six to eight months of grueling travel was closer to the truth. Days began before sunrise with breakfast, packing up tents and bedding, and hitching the animals to the wagons. After a noon break, travel continued to the next campsite—the best sites provided clean water, grass, and wood. Animals were turned loose inside a circle of wagons, cows milked, tents pitched, supper cooked and cleaned up. After enjoying a visit with fellow travelers and maybe some music around the camp fire, people headed to bed, tired from the day's journey. Throughout the trip, women struggled to keep a semblance of home and family life, but nothing about life on the trail was ordinary.

DONE BRAVE

Cooking was the most necessary daily chore. But cooking over an open camp fire was not the same as cooking on a stove back home, with familiar utensils and a full wood box close at hand. "Although there is not much to cook," lamented Helen Carpenter, "the difficulty and inconvenience in doing it, amounts to a great deal." The first shocking lesson was learning to use the plains' most abundant source of fuel—not

wood, but dried buffalo dung. Smoke constantly stung the cook's eyes, and her long skirt soon burned full of holes. Wind and rain made cooking impossible at times, forcing the family into tent or wagon to munch crackers and chew dried beef. Wild berries, fresh meat, and fish were trail treats. "One does like a change," a woman wrote, "and about the only change we have from bread and bacon is to bacon and bread." A sense of humor certainly helped.

Charlotte Pengra's journal entries kept track of her busy trail work:

> April 29, 1853...made griddle cakes, stewed berries and made tea for supper. After that was over made two loaves of bread stewed pan of apples prepared potatoes and meat for breakfast, and mended a pair of pants for William pretty tired... May 8 baked this morning and stewed apples this afternoon commenced washing...got my white clothes ready to suds...I feel very tired and lonely...May 14 gathered up the dishes and packed them dirty for the first time since I started...May 18 washed a very large washing, unpacked dried and packed clothing—made a pair of calico cases for pillows and cooked two meals—done brave, I think.

Dust coated people, animals, and possessions like a skin. Almost as thick as the dust, and more annoying, were the swarms of fleas, mosquitoes, and gnats. Weather on the journey was unpredictable and often harsh, especially when the travelers' only protection was a tent or wagon cover. "We have had all kinds of weather today," wrote Amelia Stewart Knight, who headed to Oregon in 1853 with her husband and seven children. She continued:

> This morning was dry, dusty, and sandy. This afternoon it rained, hailed, and the wind was very high. Have been traveling all the afternoon in mud and water up to our hubs. Broke chains and stuck in the mud several times.

A few weeks later she noted:

> Take us all together we are a poor looking set, and all this for Oregon. I am thinking while I write, "Oh, Oregon, you must be a wonderful country." Came 18 miles today.

Dinner on the trail

Wet weather meant wet clothes and bedding, and every so often the baggage had to be hung out to air while the wagon was cleaned and repacked. Heavy chores like this, and the most hated chore—laundry— were usually saved for a special "laying over" day, when travel stopped and work and repairs could be completed.

"THE GOING WAS TERRIBLY ROUGH"

Trail life held dangers as well as discomforts and hard work. People drowned during river crossings; children got lost or fell beneath wagon wheels; buffalo stampedes cost other lives. Disease was the emigrant's constant companion and greatest enemy. The late 1840s and early 1850s saw a worldwide cholera epidemic, and settlers carried the disease west. Victims often died within hours. Smallpox, measles, and typhoid

killed others, while dysentery, chills, and fever struck almost every traveler at some point. In June 1852, a woman observed:

> All along the road up the Platte River was a grave yard; most
> any time of day you could see people burying their dead;
> some places five or six graves in a row....It was a sad sight; no
> one can realize it unless they had seen it.

Childbirth in the middle of the wilderness proved another risk. One
girl recalled the birth of her baby sister, three days after another sister
had died:

> We were so late that the men of the party decided we could
> not tarry a day, so we had to press on. The going was terribly
> rough. We were the first party to take the southern cut-off
> and there was no road. The men walked beside the wagons
> and tried to ease the wheels down into the rough places, but
> in spite of this it was a very rough ride for my mother and her
> new born babe.

Usually sometime in July, wagon trains on the Oregon Trail crossed
the Continental Divide at South Pass, a broad, flat plain that disap-
pointed many emigrants expecting something more spectacular. The
trip was less than halfway over by this time, and the worst dangers still
lay ahead. The California route to Sacramento led through sandy desert,
terrible heat, and a climb over the Sierra Nevada range. Oregon pioneers
faced the Blue Mountains, the Cascade range, and a trip down the
mighty Columbia River before they reached the Willamette Valley.

By this stage of the journey, tension and fatigue weighed on people.
Tempers often flared and wagon trains sometimes splintered into smaller
groups. "Our company do nothing but jaw all the time," wrote one
woman. "I never saw such a cross company before." Taking an uncharted shortcut to save time looked tempting but could prove deadly.
All along the trail, furniture and tools lay abandoned to lighten the load
for exhausted animals. In the mountains, the struggle grew perilous.
Wagons had to be hoisted uphill with chains, ropes, and pulleys, then
eased down again with wheel brakes locked.

Travelers' graves along the Oregon Trail near Burnt Ranch, Wyoming. The headstones are dated 1844 and 1845.

A Mormon wagon train struggles through Echo Canyon, Utah, in 1865.

At the point where Oklahoma, Colorado, and New Mexico meet, two young western women pose for a photograph.

Oxen dropped dead in their tracks; the road was littered with dead cattle and bones bleached by the sun. "Shame on the man," exclaimed Amelia Stewart Knight,

> who has no pity for the poor, dumb brutes that have to travel and toil month after month on this desolate road. (I could hardly help shedding tears, when we drove round this poor ox who had helped us along thus far and has given us his very last step.)

"WE WOMENFOLK VISITED"

In addition to their jobs as trail homemakers, women helped with men's work, too. They drove wagons, pitched tents, loaded and unloaded, and yoked cattle. If her husband became ill, or if he died along the way, a woman had to manage on her own. One mother, on sheer willpower, got her three children through a ghastly trek in Death Valley. "All agreed," remarked one male traveler, "she was the best man of the party."

Women often relied on other females in their group for help and emotional support. They visited between wagons, spoke of old homes "back in the states," traded ideas to spice up the monotonous diet, and told of hopes for the future. They assisted with childbirth and comforted one another when needed. "Late in the afternoon," said one journal entry, "a group of women stood watching Mrs. Wilson's little babe as it breathed its last." Another woman wrote, "The female portion of our little train are almost discouraged. We sat by moonlight and discussed matters till near 11 o'clock." Exclaimed one woman, "Almira says she wished she was home, and I say ditto!" Women helped each other in other ways, too. On the treeless plains they might stand in a circle, skirts fanned out, providing one another with some privacy during calls of nature.

The months spent on the overland trails were difficult tests. Breathtaking scenery and hope existed alongside discomfort and tragedy. The trails' lessons on adapting and coping with the unexpected helped prepare women for their new lives on the frontier. Some never made it to California or Oregon. But others at last recorded thankfully in their diaries: "This is the journey's end."

OH, GIVE ME A HOME

I made a great effort to be comfortable upon very little, and simply had to do it.
—Frances Grummond,
army wife, 1866

After five months on the Oregon Trail, Amelia Stewart Knight's family arrived at their destination, greeted by rain, mud, and gloomy weather. Food prices were "all too dear for poor folks," she wrote (eggs cost one dollar a dozen), "so we have treated ourselves to some small turnips at the rate of 25 cents per dozen.

"There we are in Oregon," she continued, "making our camp in an ugly bottom, with no home, except our wagons and tent." Less than a week later, having canoed and rafted down the Columbia River and given birth to her eighth child, Amelia recorded that her husband "traded two yoke of oxen for a half section of land with one-half acre planted

to potatoes and a small log cabin and lean-to with no windows." The Knight family was home in the promised land.

Many settlers arrived in Oregon and California with little more than relief that they had survived the trip. Many were poor, ragged, thin, and sometimes disheartened. "People say they would not have staid they would go right back," wrote Martha Morrison Minto. "I would like to know how we could go back...we had no horses, nor cattle, nor anything to haul us across the plains; we had no provisions; we could not start out naked and destitute in every way."

Lucky travelers found families who had come before willing to rent them space until spring. Others continued housekeeping in wagons and tents, longing for real homes. At the very least they wanted a roof over-head and a solid floor beneath their feet. Some people dug out a hillside and burrowed in, furniture and all, until better shelter could be built. In mining camps, flimsy shacks covered with tar paper sprang up over-night. Other primitive first homes included a hollow tree stump, a cave of hay bales, and an old corncrib.

Many first homes were made of tar paper and wood.

Rough conditions were the rule. Pioneers arrived with few essential items to begin home life. One woman counted her possessions at a kettle, three knives, and two sheets. Another woman, who worked at a boardinghouse in California, complained of ankle-deep mud and described:

> All the kitchen that I have is 4 posts stuck into the ground and covered over the top with factory cloth no floor but the ground....I am scareing the Hogs out of my kitchen and Driving the mules out of my Dining room.

Homesickness permeated the early months of settlement. "i wish i was home i would give all the gold in California," wrote one woman. "i am so homesick i do not know what to do." Life was different and harsh. Said another woman, "I have cooked so much out in the hot sun and smoke that I hardly know who I am, and when I look in the little looking glass I ask, 'Can this be me?'" Despite crude conditions, many women remained hopeful. "I did not like it very well," admitted one,

A remote homestead in Homedale, Idaho

"but after we had taken our claim and became settled once more I began to like it much better and the longer I live here the better I like it."

In western areas with plentiful wood, the log cabin became the first permanent home of many settlers. Early cabins, usually only one room, lacked glass windows or a wood floor. The fireplace chimney was made of stone or sticks stuck together with clay. After the first year's crop had sold, or the family business was under way, lofts, lean-tos, floors, and window glass, as well as extra rooms, could be added.

Mud, clay, and sticks served as chinking, packed in the spaces between

A Mormon family at Farmington, Utah. For a while, some Mormons practiced polygamy—men married more than one woman. This man has several wives.

the logs. A Kansas wife recalled the rain dissolving the chinking in her house and blowing mud over everything she owned. It wasn't long, however, before the elements dried and shrank the chinking. Hot, dusty air blew through cracks in the walls during warm weather, followed by icy drafts in winter. A South Dakota woman, who claimed her log house "needed repair all the time," solved the insulation problem by surrounding her home with manure in the fall to keep it warm in winter. "When the smell got bad in the spring," she noted, "we knew it was time to take the insulation away."

HOME ON THE PLAINS

For women living on the Great Plains, the first shock was learning what sort of house they'd now be calling home. One girl recalled:

> When our covered wagon drew up beside the door of the one-roomed sod house that father had provided, he helped mother down and I remember how her face looked as she gazed about that barren farm, then threw her arms about his neck and gave way to the only fit of weeping I ever remember seeing her indulge in.

Earth was the only real building material available in many parts of the plains. Sod bricks, cut into strips about one foot wide, two feet long, and four inches thick, were stacked grassy side down to form a one-room house. Each brick weighed about 50 pounds. Boards laid over door and window openings supported more sod piled on top. Loose dirt and mud filled in between the bricks. Overhead, a frame of poles covered with brush and more sod made a roof, while underfoot was a floor of packed-down earth.

The "soddie" offered protection and insulation against heat and cold. It wouldn't burn during a deadly prairie fire. But the house was also damp, musty, and impossible to keep clean. Women tacked up yards of muslin to catch sprinklings of dirt from the walls and ceilings. In rainstorms, the soddie dripped and ran with mud. Mice, bugs, and snakes felt perfectly at home in a house made of dirt. One girl remembered from her pioneering childhood:

Sometimes the bull snakes would get in the roof and now and then one would lose his hold and fall down on the bed, and then off on the floor. Mother would grab the hoe and there was something doing and after the fight was over Mr. Bull Snake was dragged outside.

From North Dakota down to Texas, the western plains often wore a desolate and lonely face—open, arid, scoured by the wind. But the land early pioneers avoided grew more attractive with the passage of the Homestead Act in 1862. The act allowed the head of a household to pay a small filing fee on a 160-acre claim at a government land office. If the family lived on the claim and farmed it for five years, the land was theirs. Usually men, but also some single and widowed women took up the challenge.

An Oklahoma soddie

Railroad companies, which owned large tracts of western land, tempted settlers with cheap prices and advertisements promising "Land for the Landless!" and "Homes for the Homeless!" Europeans arrived in the tens of thousands to risk their chances for land. Former slaves, freed after the Civil War, came too. Some established all-black communities like Nicodemus, Kansas, and Boley, Oklahoma. "In the earliest days...," recalled a black pioneer woman, "each family was grateful for the help of each other family and 'we were all on a level.' However later differences arose and sentiment against Negros developed." Discrimination was not the only problem facing black settlers. The plains proved a brutal challenge in themselves.

Weather often arrived in extremes: heat, drought, and wind; downpours, hail, cyclones, bitter cold, and blizzards. Invasions of mosquitoes,

Schoolteachers of Guthrie, Oklahoma

Collecting buffalo dung for fuel, 1893

bedbugs, lice, and grasshoppers plagued families. For fuel, women continued burning dried buffalo or cow dung, or they twisted prairie grass into sticks. Water for chores, drinking, and cooking was in short supply. Women helped dig wells, melted snow, reused water for several tasks, and lugged it long distances from creeks or streams.

A lack of trees made life on the plains even more lonely. One woman, accompanying her husband to a distant stream to collect wood, threw her arms around a tree trunk and wept. It was the first tree she'd seen in two years. Elizabeth Custer, who followed her soldier-husband General George Custer around the West, wrote about the hardships of a land of constant glare and little shade. Nebraska author Willa Cather (1873-1947) summed up:

> Trees were so rare in that country, and they had to make such a hard fight to grow, that we used to feel anxious about them, and visit them as if they were persons. It must have been the scarcity of detail in that tawny landscape that made detail so precious.

Female homesteaders in North Dakota

Some families found the plains too much to endure and retreated east. Others hung on, finding solace in sarcastic songs such as:

> But Hurrah for Lane County, the land of the free
> The home of the grasshopper, bedbug, and flea
> I'll sing her loud praises and boast of her fame
> While starving to death on my government claim

However uninviting, land meant financial security to many people. Both women and men put up with hard work and disasters for the hope of a better future. By 1910 at least 10 percent of plains homesteaders were single women. Some, divorced or widowed, had children to support. Others had never married and came west seeking adventure and the freedom to earn their own living.

"IT DOES NOT LOOK MUCH LIKE HOME"

In all corners of the West, it was a woman's job to prepare a home and care for her family. With little to work with, western women set to their task, creating homes from adobe bricks (a mixture of clay and straw), tar paper, sod, and logs. Wrote one Kansas woman:

> The wind whistled through the walls in winter and dust blew in summer, but we papered the walls with newspapers and made rag carpets for the floors, and thought we were living well, very enthusiastic over the new country we intended to conquer.

Many frontier homes were dug out from hillsides. This Nebraska family has readied a wagonload of sod for roof repairs.

Homey touches made the difference even in a dirt house. Books were unpacked, quilts spread over beds, musical instruments placed in positions of honor. One woman had her family photographed outdoors, posing around her ornate organ. She refused to have her sod house appear in the background. Curtains seemed of special value in creating a civilized home. In some cases, women sacrificed a wedding dress or fancy petticoat and hung it at the window. Packing crates lined with calico cloth were turned into dish cupboards. Wildflowers in crocks and pitchers graced tables, and geraniums were coaxed to bloom on windowsills. Caroline Ingalls made eight major moves with her husband and four daughters. When the table was decked out in Ma's red-and-white-checked tablecloth and the china shepherdess smiled from a special bracket Pa had made, the Ingalls family knew once more they were home.

The place might have been small, poor, and cheap, but as one woman proclaimed, her two-room, tar-papered shack seemed like a palace. "For

Settlers sometimes brought all their possessions outdoors for a photograph.

Family photographs brighten the inside of a claim shack in North Dakota.

was it not my home," she asked, "after six months spent in an ox wagon?" Later, some western homes rivaled those east of the Missouri in style and comfort: frame farmhouses, Victorian homes with all the fancy trimmings, and the grand mansions of mine owners.

ARMY LIFE

While most women were trying to set down roots, army wives faced the problem of constant transfer from fort to fort. Newlywed Frances Roe cried herself sick on learning of another move. She resented leaving behind her belongings and a cherished pet dog. Many times, army families could not afford to cart all their household possessions to the next post. Women staying behind helped out, buying dishes and other goods there was no room to pack. Confided Elizabeth Custer to a friend:

> Had I ever had any housekeeping desires they would long have been quenched, so frequently do we move. What things we retain from our many movings are put down in quarters never in remarkable repair.

Army houses ranged from tents to structures described as drafty, leaky, cramped, and infested with pests from ants to rattlesnakes. Like other western wives, army women set to work improving the comfort of their homes. But just when quarters seemed homelike, an army wife might learn about the practice of "ranking out." When a new officer arrived at a fort, he claimed the best quarters his rank allowed, forcing officers of lower rank into other housing. Frances Boyd, stationed in New Mexico with her husband and three children, was bumped from a four-room house into one room by the arrival of an unmarried captain. While the captain graciously allowed the Boyds a four-week grace period since the children were ill, another army wife had only three hours to vacate her home.

Adding insult to injury, an officer's low pay had to cover food, travel, moving expenses, and other necessities. With eggs, when available, selling for $2.00 a dozen at the fort store, butter for $2.50 a pound, and kerosene fuel for $5.00 a gallon, army families remained poor and hungry. Fresh fruit, vegetables, and dairy products were seldom available. The Boyds existed on bacon, beans, flour, rice, coffee, tea, and sugar, with dried apples as a treat.

"VERY LITTLE FEMALE SOCIETY"

Most women, especially during the early months of pioneering, missed female companionship. One army wife greeted the news that four women lived at her new post: "Here we were again among women.... Hope sprang up!" A rancher's wife described her California home as beautiful, but lonely. "We were a mile from our nearest neighbor," she wrote, "and they only men. I was alone with my children most of the time for the first four months, my husband being away attending to business interests." Another woman welcomed the railroad reaching into her area, connecting her with the life and family she had known before she went west.

Sometimes months passed between visits with another woman—a white woman, that is. Native American women lived throughout the American West, and Mexican and Spanish women had lived in the

An Episcopal missionary crosses a stream on horseback, 1885.

Southwest for centuries. But white women, carting old prejudices to the frontier, were not always ready to befriend the women who already called the West home.

For many hardworking women, the lack of females in their new western home blossomed into economic opportunity. In the California mining camps especially, women's skills were in high demand. As one California pioneer excitedly planned, "A woman that can work will make more money than a man, and I think now that I shall do that."

A WOMAN THAT CAN WORK

Was I ever thrilled, seventeen years old and earning so much! I earned it all right.
—Montana schoolteacher, 1886

In 1849 Luzena Wilson arrived in a muddy California mining town with her husband and two children. Her house was a shelter of pine boughs and branches. When her husband left to round up materials for a better home, Luzena looked about and wondered what she could do to help restore the family finances. Across the way, a boardinghouse was busy serving meals. With some borrowed boards and a few stakes driven into the ground, Luzena made a table. She bought groceries from a local merchant, and when her husband returned, 20 miners sat at her table

chowing down a home-cooked meal at a dollar apiece. "From the first day it was well patronized, and I shortly after took my husband into partnership," Luzena recorded.

Women who provided miners or lonesome cowboys with homelike services—good food, clean clothes, sewing, and friendly company— could make a lot of money. Fifteen to twenty dollars a week could be had for washing clothes. One woman was paid five dollars, a princely sum in those days, for one breakfast and claimed she could have asked twice that price and been paid. Farm women made money selling such rare but longed-for items as eggs, butter, vegetables, and sewn goods like shirts, vests, and gloves. During the early days in a new western home, women often supported their families while husbands tackled mining or began farming.

Primitive conditions, however, made the backbreaking work all the harder. Mollie Sanford traveled to a Colorado silver mine with her husband and agreed to cook for the men. "My heart sinks within me," she wrote, "when I see eighteen or twenty [men], and no conveniences at all." Another woman, in 1851, listed her chores at a boardinghouse: washing, ironing, baking, cooking, setting and clearing a 30-foot-long table, feeding chickens, making soap and candles, and sewing sheets. She also baby-sat and nursed. "But I would not advise any Lady to come out here and suffer the toil and fatigue that I have suffered for the sake of a little gold," she wrote a friend back home. A California woman, proud of her hard work, said, "Had I not the constitution of six horses I should have been dead long ago."

A PAYING JOB

Women with names like Irish Queen, Peg-Leg Annie, and Contrary Mary made a living as prostitutes in mining, cattle, and railroad towns. Between 1865 and 1886, prostitution was the largest source of paid employment for women in Helena, Montana, and the story was the same in other towns as well. For some women, prostitution was just about the only way to pay the bills. Mattie Silks, a Denver prostitute, told a reporter, "I went into the sporting life for business reasons and for

no other. It was a way in those days for a woman to make money and I made it."

Other women had no choice at all. Thousands of immigrant Chinese women were sold by their poor families into prostitution and virtual slavery in the West. The problem was especially bad in San Francisco, a mining boomtown. A number of Chinese and American women tried to end the practice by rescuing young women from their "owners."

Violence, drugs, and alcohol abuse were common dangers of a life in prostitution. In the 1870s, a Virginia City, Nevada, newspaper reported that a prostitute, "age about twenty-five...committed suicide last night by drinking laudanum during a fit of despondency brought on by blighted love, acute alcoholism, and bad investments." Julia Bulette, also of Virginia City, was a favorite with the miners. She cared for the town's sick, rode through the streets in an ornate carriage, and served French wines and foods in her house. When Julia was strangled in 1867, hundreds of miners attended her funeral and the hanging of her murderer.

Of course, more respectable forms of paid employment existed for women. Jobs outside the home reflected what was considered proper work for a woman in the late 19th century. Nurturing occupations, such as teaching and domestic work, were approved of most. The sphere of suitable jobs ranged from seamstress and milliner to servant, cook, waitress, and nurse. As childbirth neared, many women trusted the services of a midwife, a fellow female, over a male doctor.

The majority of teachers in the West were unmarried women, many still teenagers. Paid little, teachers boarded with the families of their students. Schoolrooms were sometimes nonexistent; one Texas schoolmarm conducted classes outdoors under an arbor. Equipped with few supplies, teachers relied on whatever books and slates children brought from home. Pupils in a one-room school might range in age from 5 to 18 years. Sometimes, the older boys weren't about to behave for a female teacher younger than themselves.

One Kansas teacher's new schoolhouse had a cellar, but no door had yet been built to reach it. When a tornado twisted to earth and headed for her school, the teacher grabbed a firewood hatchet and chopped

Miss Crowther and her students, Central Cove, Idaho

through the floor so her students could climb down into the cellar. Luckily, the cyclone veered off in another direction. People teased the schoolmarm about scaring the tornado away with her hatchet. Discipline, they said, should come easy to her after that.

Female missionaries, of Catholic and Protestant faiths, went west to convert Native Americans to Christianity, white culture, and white values. The earliest missionaries, however committed to their calling, were hampered by their own struggle to survive in the West. One Oregon woman wrote:

> I sometimes feel discouraged and fear I shall never do anything to benefit the heathen and might as well have stayed at home....Last week I went four times to teach the Indians. But it is all I can do to get along, do my work, and take care of my children.

Newspaperwomen set type at the **Kansas Workman** *in the 1880s.*

Many western women earned their living at less traditional jobs. Some stepped in to take over the family business after the death of a husband. Others worked as reporters, typesetters, printers, artists, telegraphers, photographers, and even miners. Gender roles were less rigid in the West than they were back east. And in towns with only a handful of adult citizens, everyone was needed—male and female—to keep the post office, newspaper, and general store running.

Some women, like Helen Doyle Macknight and Bethenia Owens-Adair, became doctors. Owens-Adair married at age 14, divorced at 17, raised a child, and earned a medical degree at age 40. She paid for her education, in part, by working as a milliner and dressmaker. As a physician, Owens-Adair advised women to exercise more and wear shorter skirts. Horseback riding, a favored form of exercise, should be done astride, she argued, not sidesaddle with "the right limb twisted around a horn, and the left foot in a stirrup twelve or fifteen inches above where it ought to be."

While many African-American women in the West worked as maids or cooks, several made names for themselves as businesswomen. Biddy Mason, a slave, was taken to California by her master in 1851. California had entered the Union as a free state, and when Mason's master prepared to move again, this time to Texas, she secured the help of a Los Angeles sheriff. Through a court order, she won her right to remain in California as a free woman. Working as a nurse, Mason saved her money, then invested in building lots in Los Angeles. She earned a small fortune.

Like Biddy Mason, Clara Brown was a former slave. She worked hard as a cook and laundress, amassing a savings of $10,000. She used her earnings to help other freed slaves move west. Another African-American woman, Sallie Fingers, owned a popular restaurant in Dodge City, Kansas. In this rough-and-tumble cattle town, Fingers dared to forbid swearing, drinking, and fighting in her restaurant. The Dodge City census recorded Fingers' establishment as the only business in town owned by a woman.

Dressmakers pose with other storekeepers in an Oklahoma town.

WORKING ON THE LAND

The majority of western women made a living from the land, on their own or alongside their husbands. On a ranch, a woman usually ran the dairy side of the business. But sometimes women performed other ranch chores, from herding, branding, and cattle drives to keeping the account books. "I have tried every kind of work this ranch affords and I can do any of it," wrote a female rancher. "I just love to experiment, to prove out things, so ranch life and 'roughing it' just suits me."

Farm women lent a hand with plowing and planting and tended the farm animals. Homesteading families on the plains faced tremendous problems earning a living from the land. The sod was a tangle of thick roots that snapped plows. Wind and heat withered crops. From June 1859 until November 1860, Kansas and Nebraska faced a devastating drought that turned the land to dust and cracked the earth.

As the prairie grass dried brown under the summer sun each year, people lived with the threat of fire: huge walls of flame and smoke blackening the prairie sky and fanned by the wind. Besides plowing and clearing a trench, and lighting backfires to meet the blaze, people had little chance to fight back and often lost everything.

A North Dakota farmwife helps with spring plowing.

The Becker sisters brand cattle at their ranch in San Luis Valley, Colorado.

Millions of grasshoppers destroyed the hopes of Kansas farmers in 1874. The sky turned white as the sun caught their wings, then the grasshoppers struck the ground like hail. A writhing mass four inches deep covered everything. Not only were crops, stored grains, and trees destroyed, but the unstoppable insects also ate curtains, bedding, and food in cupboards. The green stripes on one woman's dress were eaten right off her. Nothing could be done to fight such a scourge, and the eggs the insects laid hatched the following summer to continue the devastation. No wonder many families gave up and retreated east.

"HAVE NOT SPENT AN IDLE MINUTE"

Of course, a woman's main responsibility was the never-ending work of caring for her family. Her role, carried out with few labor-saving devices, was vital to the family's survival. Chores on a given day included milking cows and feeding chickens, child care, collecting fuel and water, washing dishes, cooking, baking, churning, mending, and housecleaning. "There was always something early and late," noted a pioneer

Mother and children tend the family dairy herd in Riley County, Kansas.

woman from Texas. "When I find so much that needs to be done, I can spare very little time to sleep," wrote another.

Preparing food and preserving more for winter was a constant labor. Especially in the early days of settlement, women turned raw resources into meals without the help of store-bought provisions. Women milled grain for bread. They milked cows, skimmed cream, churned butter, and made cheese. They grew vegetables and gathered wild fruit, ground raw meat, and stuffed their own sausages.

Clothing, like food, was often created from scratch. Sheep yielded wool to be carded, spun, woven, sewn, or knitted. Laundering was a hated, backbreaking chore. Women made lye soap, hauled and boiled water in huge tubs several times over, scrubbed, rinsed, and ironed. Flatirons for pressing clothes—made out of a wedge of solid iron—were heated on the stove or fire. One woman claimed she felt like a "stewed witch" after a day

of laundry. And, as usual, even on laundry day, meals still had to be cooked, children cared for, animals tended, and much more.

Women also worked at seasonal chores like drying fruit and vegetables and making jams, candles, soap, and sausages. They helped bring in the crop and cooked huge meals for extra hands hired at harvesttime. They sheared sheep in spring and prepared cloth during long winter nights. They helped build houses, dig wells and cellars, and defend their homes against Indians and outlaws. They worked in the fields, hunted and fished, drove teams of horses into town.

Included among women's work was doctoring the family through injury and illness. Women were called on to treat everything from broken bones and fever to snakebite. Their tools were common sense,

Animal skins, heads, and antlers attest to the hunting skills of these Wyoming pioneers.

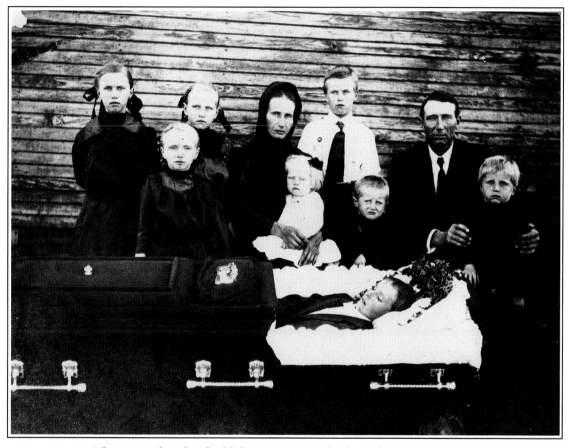

The Meget family of Oklahoma mourns the loss of a 13-year-old son.

homemade herbal remedies, and prayer. As did other aspects of western life, doctoring required some ingenuity. One Kansas woman stitched a partially scalped man with fiddle string and her sewing needle. Another time, she removed a bullet with a knitting needle and a pair of pincers.

Child care in the West presented its own set of worries. As everywhere, illness claimed young lives. But the West also delivered a high rate of accidents. Snakes, scorpions, stinging insects, and wild animals lurked where children played. A wandering child could be lost on the prairie. In mining towns, children tumbled down mine shafts and were run over in crowded streets. Mothers also feared that unsavory places

like saloons and gambling halls would corrupt their sons and daughters. An Idaho woman claimed, "This is the hardest place to live upon principle I ever saw, and the young are almost sure to be led away."

Most families grieved for the loss of at least one baby or child. A popular song of the time recalled listening for the little footsteps of a child now buried. One of a mother's most treasured possessions might be a photograph of a dead child, dressed up in the best clothes the family could provide.

Isolation from a midwife or even a neighbor woman caused some western women to fear childbirth and made recovery after birth more difficult. Frequently, mother or child died during the delivery. Martha Summerhayes, an army wife in Arizona, felt especially isolated from the comfort of other women. "I knew nothing," she wrote, "of the care of a young infant, and depended entirely upon the advice of a Post surgeon...much better versed in the sawing off of soldier's legs than in the treatment of young mothers and babies."

Overall, frontier women stretched, conserved, and made due to help their families survive. In the book *The Long Winter*, Laura Ingalls Wilder describes how her mother made a lamp from a button, a rag, and a small plate of grease. Women managed to cook custard without eggs or milk, bake apple pie without apples, brew coffee without coffee beans. Almost everyone knew what hunger was.

In the face of difficult conditions, frontier women worked hard, at home and at paying jobs, to insure the very survival of their families. No wonder then, that when the time came, everyone was ready for some fun and diversion.

AND NOW THE FUN BEGINS

Buffalo gals won't you come out
*   tonight*
and dance by the light of the
*   moon.*

—popular 19th-century
folk song

In the first years of western expansion, explorers, mountain men, and fur traders often married Native American, Mexican, and Spanish women. A fur trader found his Indian wife's wilderness know-how, as well as the help of her family, invaluable to his business. In California, white businessmen often married into well-to-do Spanish landowning families. But as increasing numbers of white women arrived west, racial prejudices caused white men to reject Indian and Hispanic women as suitable wives.

White women were in high demand, but low in numbers compared to the multitude of single men. A mining camp woman recalled that in two years she had seen only one other white woman. "Men on all sides," she reported, "but none but Indian women." Male settlers in Oregon and Washington territories advertised for brides in eastern newspapers.

In Oregon a man and his wife could each claim 320 acres of free land. The demand for brides rose dramatically. Widows remarried within a few years. Wealthy women hired homely female servants—hoping they wouldn't attract husbands of their own—only to see them married off as well. For women stuck in unhappy marriages, the odds of finding a better spouse seemed bright. One mining camp woman wrote news that probably was shocking to her sister back east:

> I tell you the women are in great demand in this country no matter whether they are married or not. you need not think strange if you see me coming home with some good looking man some of these times...it is all the go here for Ladys to leave their Husbands two out of three do it there is a first rate chance for a single woman she can have her choice of thousands.

A few women commented that the scarcity of "proper females" forced men to behave in a more chivalrous manner. "A woman on the frontier," claimed Elizabeth Custer, "is so cherished and appreciated, because she has the courage to live out there." Luzena Wilson recalled:

> Every man thought every woman in that day a beauty. Even I have had men come forty miles over the mountains, just to look at me, and I never was called a handsome woman, in my best days, even by my most ardent admirers.

KICK UP YOUR HEELS

Dancing, a favorite entertainment on the frontier, suffered during the female shortage. The first dance held in Nevada City, California, was attended by 300 men and only 12 women. A few of the men tied handkerchiefs around their arms and assumed the role of "ball-room belles" for the evening.

Dances in towns or large settlements were not complete without formal ball gowns and decorations. In other places, people shoved furniture against the wall and danced at home, with just a few instruments providing music. Sometimes, without any instrumental music, people danced to a song everyone knew, like "Skip to My Lou." Dances were

held at schools, barns, livery stables, courthouses, and on cleared patches of land. A good dance often lasted until morning light, with refreshments served at midnight. People trekked as far as 30 or 40 miles back home after breakfast.

Theater was another popular form of western entertainment, and a woman onstage often guaranteed a packed house. Cities like San Francisco and Denver boasted glittering theaters and famous talent. Fights among the customers might have been more interesting than the performance, however, if the stage was only a few boards at the back of a saloon.

Actresses willing to travel to the mining camps earned bags of gold and silver for their troubles. Miners showed up in droves to watch their favorites. Mysterious Lola Montez performed her notorious spider dance, an excuse to "kick high and shake her petticoats," claimed one observer. Caroline Chapman's repertoire included Shakespearean drama and musical comedy. A petite redhead named Lotta Crabtree charmed audiences with her spirited mandolin playing, singing, and dancing. She later conquered fans in the East and in Europe.

Known as the Frenzy of Frisco, Adah Isaacs Menken thrilled audiences

A place for entertainment in Tombstone, Arizona, 1896

with her hit play *Mazeppa.* The climactic scene featured the actress strapped to the back of a horse wearing only a skimpy robe and flesh-colored tights. Menken, a poet who could speak, read, and write four languages, earned more than $100,000 worth of gold, silver, and jewels for a single performance before the miners of Virginia City, Nevada.

"GOT ME A NEW CALICO DRESS"

Western women often claimed fashion did not matter to them. Living so far from big eastern cities, everyone wore out-of-date dresses. But in truth, a bit of finery was appreciated and saved for special occasions. Women studied eastern magazines like *Godey's Lady's Book* from cover to cover, then sought to copy the newest styles. Mail-order businesses sent yards of ribbon, lace, and braid to western seamstresses. Chinese silk shawls and scarves arrived at California ports.

Lotta Crabtree

Adah Isaacs Menken

The era of western settlement coincided with the age of hoop skirts, bustles, heavy petticoats, and waist-pinching corsets. Was fashion practical on the frontier? No, ma'am! Some women experimented with feminist Amelia Bloomer's new costume—a shorter, looser dress with baggy pants underneath, which quickly became known as "bloomers." A Kansas pioneer of 1856 found the Bloomer dress

> well suited to a wild life like mine. Can bound over the prairies like an antelope, and am not in so much danger of setting my clothes on fire while cooking when these prairie winds blow...I would not submit myself to wearing long dresses, when I can go so nimbly around...to bring water, pick up chips, bring in wood, milk.

But the Bloomer costume never caught on. Many women scorned the outfit as unfeminine. When one girl donned her father's pants to do chores, her brothers hooted with laughter, but her mother was angry. Had her daughter lost her last shred of dignity in the western wilds? Frontier women clung to fashion tradition, even if it meant wearing impractical and uncomfortable clothing. The loose-fitting dresses of Native American women, though quite modest, seemed scandalous to white women, who were laced into bone-strengthened corsets beneath pounds of clothing.

Elizabeth Custer's hoop skirts measured five yards around the bottom, and the prairie wind caused her some embarrassing moments. To outwit the elements, she sewed strips of lead into her dress hems, and "thus loaded down, we took our constitutional [walk] about the post." Another army wife admired the sensible clothing of Mexican women, who left their arms and neck bare in the southwestern heat. But at her husband's insistence, this woman sweltered in high-necked, long-sleeved summer dresses, like any well-bred woman back east in the 1870s.

A rancher described the evolution of her riding wear. For ten years she politely rode sidesaddle, dressed in a feminine riding habit. Slowly, her outfit changed. The first addition was a blue flannel shirt, followed by blue denim knickers under a short blue denim skirt. "Decadence having

By 1907 women had abandoned sidesaddles in favor of divided skirts and riding astride, as this rodeo performer demonstrates with enthusiasm.

A quilting bee in Pendroy, North Dakota, 1888

set in," she reported, "the descent from the existing standards of female modesty to purely human comfort and convenience was swift." Eventually her working clothes consisted of a shorter, split skirt, and her sidesaddle was replaced with a man's saddle.

"THE NEIGHBORHOOD ALL TURNS OUT"

No matter what shape their fashions took, western women created a busy social life for themselves as soon as possible. This was easier in towns, where women even kept up such social graces as formal visits and afternoon tea. On ranches and farms, women found ways to visit by helping one another with chores, joining in quilting bees and wool carding parties, or establishing sewing circles.

With so much work to do, women enjoyed quiet pastimes. Writing letters, scribbling in diaries, playing an instrument, singing, and embroidering all brought moments of solace and relaxation. Card parties and cribbage were popular. Books, magazines, and newspapers were read and reread, loaned, and borrowed. All across the frontier, women's literary societies met monthly to share ideas, study, and invite guest speakers.

With few books available, women set aside money to order reading materials through the mail. Army wives commented on their "precious books," while a South Dakota woman confided, "Seeing the end of my book approaching was like eating the last bit of food on my plate, still hungry, and no more food in sight."

Most western women were not afraid of the climate and western winds. They enjoyed horseback riding, fishing, and hunting. Some even tackled mountain climbing. Women studied the plants and animals of the West and recorded their findings through photographs and drawings. During the 1870s, Colorado zoologist Martha Maxwell gained a national reputation as a taxidermist.

Women's houses became special gathering places for men who longed for the comforts of home. Bachelors, on their best behavior, congregated at women's houses to eat, listen to music, play games, and visit. One mining town woman reported, "Had a spirited evening. It was exciting to meet two new gentlemen both good looking and interesting....Talked of books." On a different night, at a different house, "The jest ran high and the laughter loud. Had some good refreshments and returned home."

A mountain wedding in Colorado. The bride rides a donkey.

The Felts family enjoys a picnic in Silver City, Idaho.

Neighbors gathered at harvest parties to share work and then entertainment—dancing, good food, a cornhusking bee. In the Pacific Northwest, people met for clamming parties at the shore. Winter snows called plains pioneers outdoors for sleighing and skating. Spring and summer brought berry picking and picnics. After barn raisings, neighbors finished off the job with feasting, visiting, and maybe a dance for reward.

People traveled many miles for special celebrations. The Fourth of July was a favorite holiday in the West, crammed with horse races, picnics, speeches, parades, dances, and fireworks. Depending on the customs and traditions of a settler's heritage, a wedding might be a small gathering at home or a several-day party with suppers, songs, and dancing. Crowds assembled for special events like Court Day or political meetings. Women often spent days baking hundreds of pies and cakes for the occasions.

"THE CONGREGATION BEGAN TO GATHER"

Churches offered westerners a chance to socialize and feel part of a community. "I can see all the neighbors twice a week," confided one woman, "for we have prayer meeting Thursday evenings." People longed for the familiar habits of life back east, and building a church was an important step. Many western settlements, however, did not have enough families or money to support a church. Instead settlers looked forward to the arrival of a traveling preacher. Camp meetings, which lasted for days, involved preaching, singing, and conversions to the faith. People came from miles around and camped out to be part of the worship and social excitement. One Oregon woman hosted a 10-day-long prayer meeting at her house. "Our one room," she wrote, "served for church, kitchen, dining room, bedroom and study for the preachers, sometimes we had three or four as they came from adjoining circuits to help us through the week." Wrote another woman, "We looked forward to the camp meeting in June....I think they were pretty nearly our only salvation from entire stagnation."

In all areas of the West, women sought the joy in life to match their hard work. Fun was often found in simple things and friendly company.

The "gospel wagon" brought religion to rural communities.

GREAT EXPECTATIONS FOR THE FUTURE

That every woman of the age of twenty one years, residing in this Territory, may, at any election...cast her vote.

—Wyoming Territory legislation, December 1869

The West grew quickly. Towns with crowded dirt streets and a hodge-podge of hastily nailed together buildings provided goods and services for miners, cattlemen, and farmers. Violence was never in short supply. "In the short space of twenty-four days, we have had murders, fearful accidents, bloody deaths, a mob, whippings, a hanging, an attempt at suicide and a fatal duel," reported a female resident of a California mining town. Another woman described her shock and grief when the Sabbath was shattered by the hanging of two men. Women enjoyed the benefits of town life—shopping, socializing, and job opportunities—but the lawless ways had to change.

In the 19th century, a woman's role was to raise her children, comfort those in need, and provide a home in which her husband could retreat from his daily cares. Preserving the "moral values" of society also rested on a woman's shoulders. For the West, the American Missionary Society prescribed:

> We must send no more unmarried men. California needs woman's influence...a devoted intelligent woman can do more than two ministers. A shipload of female missionaries would be the greatest blessing California ever had.

In the American East and South, the lives of middle- and upper-class women grew more and more restrictive during the 19th century. In the view of one male writer, women naturally shrank from the struggle and competition of life. Like a child, he wrote, a woman "has but one right and that is the right to protection. The right to protection involves the obligation to obey." Throughout much of the 19th century, women held no legal right to vote, own property, or gain custody of their children.

Frontier women lacked these rights, but they might have laughed at the notion that they needed protection and shrank from life's struggle. Western women did not sit back demurely and leave the job of settling western lands to the men. There was too much to accomplish—often survival itself was at stake. Women, wrote a Kansas female, "learned at an early age to depend upon themselves to do whatever work there was to be done, and to face danger when it must be faced."

While the West produced its share of notorious ladies, like barroom brawler Calamity Jane and the outlaw Belle Starr, most women who lent a hand settling the frontier were ordinary people. Women and men both believed that frontier rawness needed reform. Men, however, could initiate change through their vote and by holding public office. Without political rights, women found other ways to push for change.

As the art of sheer survival gave way to a more settled life, women looked around and found important elements missing from the western scene. If a woman's role was to civilize, she would start with the things closest to her heart. Schools and churches stood at the top of the list.

SCHOOL'S IN SESSION

Many women believed that schools would help civilize the rough frontier. When too few families lived in an area to support a school, mothers taught their children at home or sent them to a neighbor woman for instruction. Lessons included reading, writing, and math, with a good dose of morality thrown in as well. Some westerners—especially army families—made sacrifices to send their children back east for an education.

As soon as enough school-age children lived in a county, parents banded together to form school systems. Women, traveling on horseback or driving wagons, collected signatures of support for the schools and wrote letters to county and state superintendents. Tax moneys didn't always cover the cost of teachers' salaries and schoolhouses. So women made up for the shortfall with fund-raisers like box suppers and theatricals. Parents themselves often built the schoolhouse when an existing building or room could not be found, and families welcomed

Sargent County school, North Dakota

teachers as boarders in their homes. One South Dakota woman, a teacher before marriage, said, "Just having a school available made life look a lot better to me."

By organizing schools, many women entered public affairs for the first time. If women could help establish schools and work in them as teachers, they asked, why shouldn't they have a vote on school taxes, bonds, and school board elections? Why shouldn't a woman sit on the school board or be elected superintendent of schools?

Nebraskan Luna Kellie first asked such questions when local men without children tried to cut the length of the school term to save taxes. "Right then," said Kellie,

> I saw for the first time that a woman might be interested in politics and want a vote. I had been taught that it was unwomanly to concern oneself with politics and that only the worst class of women would ever vote if they had a chance etc etc but now I saw where a decent mother might wish very much to vote on local affairs at least.

In 1861 Kansas became the first state to allow women to vote in school elections.

TIME FOR RELIGION

From the days of the Oregon Trail, Christian women deplored the lack of religion in western life. "And today is Sunday again," wrote a western-bound woman. "O what Sundays. There is nothing that seems like the Sabbath." Women missed the comfort and strength found in religious services. Many feared for their children's well-being, raised without a church and knowing the benefit of a traveling minister's visit only three or four times a year. Bible reading at home could not replace weekly worship with others. As they had with schools, women often took the lead in raising funds to build local churches and hire ministers. One woman took three boarders into her home so she might contribute to her community's church-building coffers. Women opened their homes for church services and prayer meetings, taught Sunday school to children, and oversaw charity work.

Other groups brought their faith to the frontier. By 1852 about 20,000 Mormon settlers were busy building their own Zion at Salt Lake City, Utah. Mormon women, many of whom had trekked across the plains for religious freedom, served their church with devotion and supported the Mormon religion throughout Utah Territory and the West. Small numbers of Jewish women also went west. Most had emigrated from Europe, mainly Bavaria or Poland, to escape religious persecution and economic hardship. Many western Jews moved not to farms but to towns, where they had a better chance of organizing a synagogue with other Jewish families and hiring a rabbi. Women founded groups like the Hebrew Ladies' Benevolent Society to assist other Jewish settlers with loans and advice.

"AIMING FOR BETTER COMMUNITIES"

Throughout the West, Ladies Aid societies undertook fund-raising and charity activities. Thousands of women's clubs pledged to work for community improvement. Women founded libraries, donating books and volunteer hours to keep them open. Money raised through bazaars, box suppers, and socials helped widows and orphans, provided scholarships for female students, and aided the poor. Black women also organized clubs, such as the Sojourner Truth Club of Los Angeles and the Sisters of Ethiopia, that served the African-American community.

Women also sent aid to starving farm families, devastated by drought or grasshopper invasions. Male community leaders sometimes opposed this work, fearing that calling attention to such problems would keep new settlers from the territory. In one Kansas town, women sent a letter to their local newspaper, offering to take the men to see the devastation firsthand. It would hurt Kansas's image more, argued the women, to let settlers die of starvation. That said, they gathered food and clothing to help the farmers.

Women's reform efforts began spilling into political areas as well. The first issue to unite large numbers of women was the question of temperance—abstention from alcohol. Much of the West's violence stemmed from male drunkenness. Women, in their role as "protector of family

and society," focused on alcohol's power to destroy. As early as the 1850s, some women demanded that saloons close on Sundays. To this end, women's groups collected signatures and held public meetings.

In 1874 the Women's Christian Temperance Union was founded in Ohio; by 1890 the WCTU was the largest women's organization in the United States. In 1878 Kansas alone had 26 local chapters. Kansan Carry Nation, whose first husband died of alcoholism, became the most famous temperance advocate in the country. Nation felt called upon by God to fight the "Demon Rum." Armed with a hatchet, she invaded saloons, smashing bottles, mirrors, and furniture.

Most temperance supporters, however, used less violent means to call attention to the issue. They carried banners blazoned with slogans such as "Tremble King Alcohol, I shall grow up." Temperance workers gave lectures, wrote songs, lobbied state legislatures, passed out pamphlets, and sponsored essay contests in schools about the curse of alcohol. Their work eventually led to the passage of the 18th Amendment, which—for a time—prohibited the manufacture and sale of alcoholic beverages throughout the United States.

Temperance crusader
Carry Nation

"I COULD, I CAN, AND I DO"

Many women active in temperance work and other civic projects joined another growing movement—the fight for women's suffrage, the right to vote. Opponents argued that female suffrage would strip women of their femininity, destroy familes, and go against the laws of God.

Though the battle for women's rights originated in the East during the 1840s, the first real gains came in the West. By 1861 women in Kansas had won the right to vote in school elections and to hold property in their own names. An attempt in 1867 to grant women full suffrage in Kansas attracted national attention. Eastern suffrage leaders like Elizabeth Cady Stanton, Lucy Stone, and Susan B. Anthony traveled west to support the cause. The bitter battle was lost, however, and Kansas women did not receive the vote in national and state elections until 1912. They did gain the right, in 1887, to vote and run for office in city elections.

Wyoming women, on the other hand, quietly won the right to vote without rallies, petitions, or conventions. Perhaps influenced by his wife and 56-year-old Esther Morris, territorial senator William Bright introduced a bill to the Wyoming legislature in November 1869. The bill read that every woman age 21 and older would have the right to vote and hold office. Before opposition could organize, the bill passed on December 10 and was signed into law by the governor.

So, in Wyoming, on September 6, 1870, women turned out at the polls and exercised their legal right to vote for the first time in history. Earlier that year, Esther Morris was appointed a justice of the peace, and Wyoming became the first territory to select women for jury duty. Eastern newspapers ridiculed the idea, running a cartoon that showed women chomping cigars and nursing their babies in a jury box. The caption read, "Baby, baby don't get in a fury, your mother's going to sit on a jury." But the judge in charge of the first trial with female jurors assured the women they would not be driven from their duty by "jeers and insults of a laughing crowd." Their right was protected by law. In 1890 Wyoming entered the Union as the first state to include state and national voting rights for women in its constitution.

Campaigning for the vote in Colorado

At a rally for suffrage in New York City, demonstrators bear shields naming states where women have won the vote—all in the West.

Other suffrage struggles ended in defeat. Utah women won the vote in 1870 and lost it in 1877. After losing their bid for suffrage in 1877, Colorado women won the vote in 1893, followed in 1896 by the women of Idaho and, again, Utah. By 1914, 11 of the last 18 states to join the Union—all of them in the West—had guaranteed women's suffrage, while none of the first 30 states had. Perhaps the difference was the West's newness. It was easier to write new laws than to repeal long-standing ones. Susan B. Anthony wrote to a Utah newspaper in 1894:

> Now in the formative period of your constitution is the time to establish justice and equality to all the people....Once ignored in your constitution—you'll be powerless to secure recognition as are we in the older states.

Perhaps another reason suffrage succeeded in the West was the support given to the movement by a new grassroots political party. The

Populist Party, which championed the rights of farmers and other working people, enjoyed a strong following out west in the 1880s and 1890s. Women flocked to the Populist cause and for the first time played an important role in a major political party.

One of the most famous voices of the Populist movement belonged to Mary Lease, a Kansan who began her speaking career in the Farmers' Alliance. In 1890 alone, Lease made more than 160 speeches to thousands of men and women. She held railroad companies and Wall Street bankers responsible for the farmer's financial troubles. "What the farmers need," she told one audience, "is to raise less corn and more hell!" For her efforts, the eastern press dubbed her the "Pythoness of Kansas" and Mary "Yellin" Lease.

Western newspapers noted women's involvement in politics and reported, "Women who never dreamed of becoming public speakers, grew eloquent in their zeal and fervor." Women, said another paper, "could talk straight to the point." And political humorist Joseph Billings commented, "Wimmin is everywhere."

Western women reflected on their own accomplishments. As one mining town woman wrote to her sister in Massachusetts, she had sent her roots into the barren western soil and "gained an unwonted strength in what seemed to you such unfavorable surroundings."

CLASH OF CULTURES

My people talked fearfully that winter about those they called our white brothers.

—Sarah Winnemucca

Where white pioneer women saw an unforgiving wilderness, Native American women saw a loved and familiar home. From the Great Plains and Rocky Mountains to the southwestern desert and the forests of the Pacific Northwest, Native American women lived very differently from the white newcomers. Indian tribes in each region also lived differently from one another—with different languages, religions, types of homes, styles of clothing, and food.

Native American women harvested plants and crops and turned them into items needed for survival—food, clothing, and shelter. Though many Indian men hunted for meat and protected the tribe, a group's

Nez Perce women on horseback

well-being depended heavily on women's work. Like white women, Indian women's contributions revolved around home and children.

Life was difficult, especially for tribes living in desert areas where food was sometimes scarce. In many Indian societies, distributing food was a woman's job. The tribe respected a generous woman; food hoarding was a serious offense. A guest was always offered food as a symbol of welcome.

A woman's knowledge of edible plants helped her gather fruits, nuts, seeds, roots, and herbs. In farming tribes, women tended and harvested

A Cheyenne woman constructs a tipi.

crops and preserved food for winter. Among the Hopi and Zuni people of the Southwest, women owned the fields and men often worked them. At harvesttime, women took charge, drying and grinding vast amounts of corn into meal. Kneeling before the grinding stone for hours at a time, women murmured prayers and songs of thanks for the good harvest. Grinding 25 pounds of cornmeal was considered a good day's work. The meal was shared with relatives who had no daughters to help them.

Butchering and drying meat—no small feat after a buffalo hunt—was the job of plains women. Speed was important so the meat would not spoil. If her husband or father was a good hunter, a woman might be faced with 20 buffalo carcasses to process and tan. Dressing a buffalo hide took three to six days and involved pegging the skin flat, scraping off the fat and tissue, treating the hide with chemicals (made from the animal's brain, liver, and fat), and working it into a soft usable material.

Plains women sewed their homes from buffalo skins; a large tipi needed about 22 hides. Like white settlers, Indian women called on one another

for assistance in building their homes, and they prepared a feast for everyone who helped with the work. The finished tipi, and all the furnishings and equipment inside, belonged to the woman. Whenever the tribe moved, she was responsible for taking down, packing, unpacking, and setting up the tipi at its new location. Women in other regions also built the family home: the Navajo hogan, the Apache wickiup, the mud bricks and adobe apartments of the Pueblo peoples.

Women prepared all their family's clothing from animal skins or materials woven from wool, softened bark, and grasses. Leather moccasins or sandals protected their feet. Tribes living in northern climates added leggings and a buffalo-skin robe for winter.

Many Indian women owned not only the property they brought into a marriage but anything they made afterward: tools, utensils, bags, and

Navajo women were in charge of the sheep and goat herds.

*An Apache woman
outfitted in beads and
traditional dress*

storage containers. Indian women did not waste time making decorative items that served no useful purpose. But they expressed their talents and creativity by turning everyday objects into things of beauty. In some tribes, a woman's skill in decorative arts was esteemed like a warrior's deeds in battle.

Southwestern peoples like the Paiute, Navajo, Pima, Papago, and Apache excelled at making tightly woven baskets. Fabric weaving was an art form among the tribes of the Pacific Northwest and the Navajo of the

Southwest. Navajo weaving was said to originate with Spider Woman, a legendary figure who long ago taught the art to her people. Because women owned and tended the Navajo sheep and goat herds, they had economic power that many other Indian women (and white women) lacked.

The Pueblo women of the Southwest made beautiful pottery, often with walls as thin as eggshells. One Zuni woman claimed she painted all her thoughts onto her pottery. Nomadic plains tribes needed more durable items. Plains women used buffalo hides to make everything from storage bags to cradleboards to clothing and moccasins. These were then decorated with beads and dyed porcupine quills in many colors and designs. Beads were formed of bone, shell, animal teeth, nuts, seeds, stones, and, later, glass received from white traders. Skilled Cheyenne women belonged to an exclusive quilling society, which taught the art to younger women.

Like white pioneer women, Indian women enjoyed socializing and recreation. Dances celebrated successful harvests, hunts, and battles and played a part in religious ceremonies. Some tribes held dances as a way for young men and women to meet. Whereas white society thought physical strength made a woman unfeminine, the strongest, healthiest Indian women were respected as good workers and mothers. Indian women swam, raced horses, and sledded in winter. Cheyenne women played a kind of football. Pima and Papago women loved field hockey. Balls were fashioned from hide stuffed with grass or animal hair. More quiet pastimes included string games, like cat's cradle, and gambling games using dice.

Religion was woven into the very fabric of an Indian woman's life. The forces of life and death were everywhere to be seen—in the seasons, the hunt, the planting, and the harvest. Prayers asked for food and good health for the tribe. In some tribes, women, as well as men, hoped for a vision or special dream to show them the road to a good life. Many native cultures revered female spirits, like White Buffalo Calf Woman, who brought the sacred pipe to the Lakota and taught them to live as one with all creatures, the earth, and the sky.

In many tribes, women gained power and honor with age. Passing on the wisdom of a lifetime, they offered advice about tribal matters, history, religion, and medicines. Children listened with respect while elders taught the ways and stories of their people. Some tribes had female chiefs, usually mature women who had won distinction through their generosity and hard work.

Three generations of Kiowa women

Indian women gained status through other roles as well. A medicine woman earned both respect and wealth. Her tools included special songs, prayers, and herbal treatments made from mosses, roots, bark, and leaves. Bravery was an attribute admired—and expected—from women as well as men. Some women followed men to war as cooks and nurses. Other women, like Yellow Haired Woman of the Cheyenne or He-e-e, the warrior girl of the Hopi, defended their villages from attack. A strong-minded woman was called "manly hearted" by the Blackfeet tribe.

"WE EYED THEM WITH A GOOD DEAL OF CURIOSITY"

Indian women viewed the white people coming into their lands with both fear and curiosity. Mothers thought their children would be stolen or murdered by the strangers. White people's food, to Indian taste, had no strength. The pale-skinned females wore ridiculous clothes and shoes. What shape was hiding beneath those hoop skirts and bustles? Indian society especially could not understand the white settlers' desire to possess land and to change it to suit their needs. One Indian woman claimed she learned nothing useful or helpful from the newcomers.

White women heading west in the 1840s also were curious and fearful about the native people they encountered. First meetings were usually friendly, though some women were not impressed with the Indians' appearance—"painted, dirty, nauseous-smelling savages," wrote one. Descriptions such as "treacherous," "thieving," and "bloodthirsty" appear in white women's journals. Emigrant women did not understand that in most Indian societies visitors exchanged gifts. Instead, when Indians expected food or gifts from the newcomers, white women condemned them for what they thought was begging.

Their journals noted, however, how the Indians could be of help: "I traded an apron today for a pair of moccasins of the Indians." "We have engaged our passage down the Columbia this morning in a canoe with the Indians." "Have also a good many Indians and bought fish of them. They all seem peaceful and friendly." "Quite a number of Indians were camped around us, for the purpose of selling salmon to the emigrants." One woman advised that new settlers pack a supply of calico shirts to trade.

But white women, often alone on their homesteads, feared the sudden appearance of curious Indians at their cabin doors. "These Osage are said to be friendly," wrote one woman, "but I cannot look at their painted visages without a shudder." She clutched her children to her side, afraid the Indians would steal them. If provoked, a white woman would defend her home and family, though her weapon might be nothing more than a broom. Unwelcome Indian visitors usually retreated. For the most part, when fear died down, white women viewed Indians as people to be pitied—inferior, they believed, to the white race.

White women journeying west heard lurid tales of what happened to females captured by Indians. George Custer ordered that in case of attack, any man near Elizabeth was to shoot her instead of letting her fall into Indian hands. A young woman named Olive Oatman survived a slavelike captivity with the Mohave tribe and bore the tattoos she received for the rest of her life.

Some female captives did not want to be rescued from their Indian life, however. From age 9, when she was stolen, until age 34, Cynthia Ann Parker lived as a Comanche on the southern plains. In 1860 she was captured by government Indian hunters and was returned to her white relatives. Though she kept her baby daughter, Parker longed for the sons and husband she'd left behind. Several times she tried to escape and return to her Comanche family. Four years later, when her daughter died, Parker starved herself to death. Her son Quanah became a famous Comanche chief.

Anna Morgan lived out her 1868 captivity as the wife of a Sioux chief. She described, "I began to think much of him for his kindness to me, and when they brought the news that there were two white men in the camp, I did not care to see them." Nevertheless, she was returned to her former life and bore the chief's son several months later. The child died and Morgan wrote, "After I came back, the road seemed rough, and I often wished they had never found me." White people believed women like Morgan feared returning, not because they had come to respect and prefer Indian society, but because of their shame and disgrace from living among the "savages."

"THE WHITE PEOPLE HAVE TAKEN"

As the trickle of white pioneers turned into hundreds of thousands, the clash between Indian and white cultures grew more violent. Native Americans watched their children die from white people's diseases, saw the buffalo and other food destroyed. Indian villages, including women, children, and old people, were attacked by blue-coated soldiers. Ragged bands of Indians were hunted until they surrendered to life on reservations. Indian women felt the wrenching pain of loss. Recalled one Cheyenne woman:

> I used to cry every time anything reminded me of the killing of my husband and my son. I used to hate all white people, especially the soldiers. But my heart has become changed to softer feelings. Some of the white people are good, maybe as good as Indians.

At Indian boarding schools, like this one near Fort Defiance, Arizona, Native American children were forced to learn English and adopt the dress and customs of white Americans.

In 1886 the last free band of Native Americans—Geronimo's Apaches —surrendered to white soldiers. Like other western tribes, the Apaches were rounded up and driven onto reservation lands, often hundreds of miles from their well-loved homelands. Once proud cultures suffered. Children were taken away to boarding schools, where Indian language and customs were degraded. The U.S. government banned Indian dances, ceremonies, and religious practices. Hunting was forbidden. For men considered brave hunters and warriors, reservation life was empty and meaningless. With hunting banned and with government-issued cloth to sew, women's traditional tanning and quilling skills declined. Overall, however, the rhythm of life did not change as sharply for Indian women as it did for men. Children still needed raising, food cooking, clothes sewing, homes kept. Many times, Indian women preserved their tribal heritage. "A nation is not conquered," went a Blackfeet saying, "until the hearts of its women are on the ground."

The early reservation years were especially difficult for people used to freedom and food enough to feed themselves. Corruption polluted the reservation system. Government agents sold food and clothing meant for the Indians. They allowed whites to squat on the best reservation lands. For thousands of Indian people, reservation life brought starvation and mistreatment.

During the early 1880s, two Indian women, a Paiute named Sarah Winnemucca and an Omaha named Susette La Flesche, gained national prominence fighting the injustice shown their people. Both women spoke English, and La Flesche had been educated in the East. Dressed in traditional Indian costumes, which white audiences thought exotic, they lectured in eastern cities, wrote books, and traveled to Washington, D.C., to speak on behalf of Native Americans.

Sarah Winnemucca pleaded for an end to the terrible treatment of reservation Indians, especially her own people. "The women," she wrote of Paiute society, "know as much as the men do, and their advice is often asked." She chastised white legislators by writing, "If women could go into your Congress, I think justice would soon be done to the Indians."

Susette La Flesche lectured whites about years of broken treaties and the theft of Indian lands. She decried the fact that Indians were not even considered persons before the law, and she battled for citizenship and equal rights for Indians. In a letter to the Indian Commission she wrote:

> It's all a farce when you say you are trying to civilize us, then, after we educate ourselves, refuse us positions of responsibility and leave us utterly powerless to help ourselves.

Susette La Flesche and her brother Francis

FINDING COMMON GROUND

Most white settlers never tried to understand the native people whose lands they stole and whose lives they destroyed. But some white women did make an effort. Army wives, who saw the Indians' conditions first-hand, voiced sympathy. Frances Roe realized that "If the Indians should attempt to protect their rights it would be called an uprising at once." All they could do was watch helplessly while the buffalo were destroyed, she continued, "and all the time they know only too well that with them will go the skins that give them tepees and clothing, and the meat that furnishes almost all of their sustenance." Another army wife, whose husband died fighting the Sioux, felt it was clear that "the Indians...would fight to the death for home and native land...and who would say that their spirit was not commendable and to be respected?" Many female pioneers gave what food and clothing they could to local Indians and hired them to help around their farms. Other women worked as teachers or missionaries on Indian reservations.

In general, white women had peaceful relationships with Indians. When coming face to face as women, they probably discovered more in common with their Native American sisters than they liked to admit. One missionary described how Indian women helped her cope after childbirth. Another white woman claimed she only survived the loneliness of her western home because some Indian women had befriended her. She later returned their friendship by hiding them from drunken soldiers. When the tribe moved on, the Indian women presented her with a small ring. "No words can express," she claimed, "what that little gold ring meant to me, the love and kindly feeling that was in the hearts of those three Indian women has been a very precious memory to me."

As white people swept across the continent and gobbled up new lands, they didn't worry about whose lands they claimed. Many believed it was the destiny of the United States to rule North America from the Atlantic to the Pacific. Racial prejudices made the job easy. The scramble for elbow room and riches came at the expense of Mexican Americans as well as Native Americans. Whites stole cattle from Mexican ranchers. They cheated Mexican landowners out of their property using high taxes and

***Mexican Americans throughout the Southwest lost their lands to white
settlers.***

complicated laws written in English. Threats and violence scared other
Mexicans off their land. In letters, Hispanic women labeled the greedy
Americans as "thieves," "murderers," and people "not to be trusted."

By 1848 war and treaties had forced Mexico to hand over Texas,
California, and New Mexico to the United States. A settlement with
Great Britain gave the United States all of Oregon Country below the
49th parallel. Huge numbers of white settlers had arrived and were in
the West to stay. And more kept coming. By 1890 so many people had
sought the promise of a better life in the West that historians called the
American frontier officially "closed."

LOVE SONG TO THE WEST

*How often at night
    when the heavens are bright
With the lights from the
    glittering stars
Have I stood here amazed
    and asked as I gazed
If their glory exceeds that
    of ours*

> —second verse,
> "Home on the Range"

As a new bride, Frances Boyd regarded her New York City home as "the only habitable place on the globe." In 1868, however, she joined her soldier-husband in the wild Southwest. Seventeen years later, a life of privation and hardship could not dampen Boyd's appreciation for the West. "Oh, I love the West," she wrote, "and dislike to think that the day will surely come when it will teem with human life and all its warring elements!"

On a year-long visit back to New York, Boyd "raved about the de-lights of the West until friends thought me nearly crazy on the subject." She proclaimed New York's Catskill Mountains "insipid after the rocky grandeur of the west" and deplored New York City's endless turmoil and chimneys blocking out the sky. Years later, returning east as a widow, Frances Boyd never forgot the blue-domed skies and grand spaces of the Southwest, where, she wrote, "one is truly alone with God."

Many women echoed Boyd's celebration of beauty, freedom, and joy in the West. "The air is so exhilarating," wrote Elizabeth Custer, "one

A North Dakota homesteader at the water pump

Western daredevils celebrate atop a peak in Yosemite Valley, California.

feels as if he had never breathed a full breath before." A Kansas woman described her new home in 1859:

> It was such a new world, reaching to the far horizon without break of tree or chimney stack; just sky and grass and grass and sky....The hush was so loud. As I lay in my unplastered upstairs room, the heavens seemed nearer than ever before and awe and beauty and mystery over all.

"It might seem a cheerless life," claimed another woman,

> but there were many compensations: the thrill of conquering a new country; the wonderful atmosphere; the attraction of the prairie, which simply gets into your blood and makes you dissatisfied away from it; the low-lying hills and the unobstructed view of the horizon; and the fleecy clouds driven by the never failing winds.

Award-winning author Willa Cather portrayed the western land as a powerful force in her stories. Many pioneering women shared the same tug at their souls, the sense of themselves, the sense of change, that Cather expressed:

> It was over flat lands like this, stretching out to drink the sun, that the larks sang—and one's heart sang there, too....There was a new song in that blue air which had never been sung in the world before.

SELECTED BIBLIOGRAPHY

Armitage, Susan, and Jameson, Elizabeth, eds. *The Women's West.* Norman: University of Oklahoma Press, 1987.

Bartley, Paula, and Loxton, Cathy. *Plains Women: Women in the American West.* Cambridge: Cambridge University Press, 1991.

Boyd, Frances. *Cavalry Life in Tent and Field. 1894.* Reprint. Lincoln: University of Nebraska Press, 1982.

Brown, Dee. *The Gentle Tamers: Women of the Old Wild West.* Lincoln: University of Nebraska Press, 1958.

Capps, Benjamin. *The Indians.* The Old West series. New York: Time-Life Books, 1973.

Carrington, Frances. *My Army Life.* 1910. Reprint. Boulder, Colorado: Pruett Publishing Co., 1990.

Custer, Elizabeth. *Boots and Saddles, or Life in Dakota with General Custer.* 1885. Reprint. Norman: University of Oklahoma Press, 1961.

_____. *Tenting on the Plains.* Norman: University of Oklahoma Press, 1971.

Fischer, Christiane, ed. *Let Them Speak for Themselves: Women in the American West 1849-1900.* Hamden, Connecticut: Archon Books, 1977.

Gray, Dorothy. *Women of the West.* Millbrae, California: Le Femmes Press, 1976.

Horn, Huston. *The Pioneers.* The Old West series. New York: Time-Life Books, 1974.

Jeffrey, Julie. *Frontier Women: The Trans-Mississippi West 1840-1880.* New York: Hill and Wang, 1979.

Luchetti, Cathy, and Olwell, Carol. *Women of the West.* New York: Orion Books, 1982.

Merington, Marguerite, ed. *The Custer Story: The Life and Intimate Letters of General George A. Custer and His Wife Elizabeth.* New York: The Devin-Adair Co., 1950.

Myres, Sandra. *Westering Women and the Frontier Experience 1800-1915.* Albuquerque: University of New Mexico Press, 1982.

Niethammer, Carolyn. *Daughters of the Earth: Lives and Legends of American Indian Women.* New York: MacMillan Publishing Co., Collier Books, 1977.

Riley, Glenda. *The Female Frontier.* Lawrence: University Press of Kansas, 1988.

Roe, Frances. *Army Letters from an Officer's Wife.* 1909. Reprint. Lincoln: University of Nebraska Press, 1981.

Schlissel, Lillian. *Women's Diaries of the Westward Journey.* New York: Schocken Books, 1982.

Stratton, Joanna. *Pioneer Women: Voices from the Kansas Frontier.* New York: Simon and Schuster, 1981.

Summerhayes, Martha. *Vanished Arizona: Recollections of My Army Life.* 1908. Reprint. New York: J. B. Lippincott Co., 1963.

Wallace, Robert. *The Miners.* The Old West series. New York: Time-Life Books, 1976.

Wyman, Walker. *Frontier Women: The Life of a Woman Homesteader on the Dakota Frontier.* River Falls: University of Wisconsin Press, 1972.

INDEX

ACKNOWLEDGMENTS

Photographs and illustrations used with permission of the Denver Public Library, Western History Department: pp. 2, 9, 10, 30, 34, 49 (both), 53, 63, 64, 75; Starsmore Center for Local History, Colorado Springs Pioneers Museum: pp. 6, 55; New York Historical Society, New York City: p. 7; Laura Westlund: p. 12; Kansas State Historical Society: pp. 15, 27, 38, 42, 68; Wyoming State Museum: pp. 17 (top), 23, 43, 80; Church Archives, The Church of Jesus Christ of Latter-day Saints: p. 17 (bottom); Western History Collections, University of Oklahoma Library: pp. 18, 25, 26, 33, 39, 44, 48, 51, 61, 72, 84; Nebraska State Historical Society: pp. 20, 29, 77; State Historical Society of North Dakota: pp. 21, 28, 31, 40, 52, 58, 81; Idaho State Historical Society: pp. 22 (Photo No. 3201-A), 37 (Photo No. 79-63.2), 54 (Photo No. 12-155.23), 67 (Photo No. 694); Colorado Historical Society: pp. 41 (Neg. #F28,537), 46 (Neg. #F41276), 56, 69 (Neg. #F42,582), 79 (Neg. #F33,148), 86, 88; Nevada Historical Society: p. 66; U.S. Signal Corps, National Archives: p. 70; National Park Service, Yosemite National Park: p. 82.

Front cover: Nebraska State Historical Society Back cover: Nevada State Museum, Carson City